CHICAGO'S PASSENGER TRAINS

—A GALLERY OF PORTRAITS 1956-1981—

ROBERT P. OLMSTED

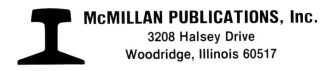

McMILLAN PUBLICATIONS, Inc.
3208 Halsey Drive
Woodridge, Illinois 60517

CHICAGO'S PASSENGER TRAINS

Copyright © 1982 by Robert P. Olmsted and McMillan Publications
Printed and bound in U.S.A.
Photography/Robert P. Olmsted
Halftones/Jim Walter Graphic Arts—Beloit, Wisconsin
Printing/Terry Printing—Janesville, Wisconsin
Typesetting/Guetschow Typesetters—South Beloit, Illinois
Binding/Zonne Bookbinders—Chicago, Illinois

ISBN 0-934228-10-8

Library of Congress Catalog Card Number: 82-62562

First Printing—February 1983

Second Printing—September 1983

Third Printing—October 1984

TO CHARLES KRUBL

Right . . . Crossroads of the Midwest—the diamonds at 21st Street in Chicago. In the summer of 1966, Santa Fe 22 accelerates the westbound *Grand Canyon* toward California and three Pennsylvania E's begin their journey to New York with the *Manhattan Limited.* Dearborn Station's other occupants (in addition to the Santa Fe) all curved south (right in the photos) at this point. The Illinois Central's Iowa-bound trains followed the same steel path being negotiated by the Santa Fe's A-B-B-A team.

Front end sheet . . . On the last day of December 1969, the Burlington/Northern Pacific's *North Coast Limited* curves across the snow-covered Illinois landscape a mile east of Sugar Grove.

Back end sheet . . . Nearing the Aurora stop, Burlington Northern's *Denver Zephyr* charges through West Eola at sunset in March 1970. On this March 14th, the BN merger is two weeks old, the *California Zephyr* has only one more week to run and Amtrak still is a year away.

Title page . . . At sixty and increasing, Pullmans of the *Pacific*-series are urged west across Illinois in the consist of Milwaukee/Union Pacific's #105/111, the combined *City of Portland/City of Denver.*

CHICAGO'S PASSENGER TRAINS—Every few minutes in the 1950's, a passenger train arrived or departed one of Chicago's six major terminals (from east to west—Illinois Central, Dearborn, La Salle, Grand Central, Union and North Western). By 1970 only a handful of these trains survived. On the following pages, recall the great trains of Chicago, some last runs, a few survivors, and then the emergence of Amtrak.

Dearborn, Chicago's oldest station dating from 1885, hosted the greatest variety of passenger trains of all of the Windy City's great temples of transportation. In the late 1950's, six roads called Dearborn home, the Chicago & Eastern Illinois, Erie, Grand Trunk Western, Monon, Santa Fe and Wabash. On a July 1958 morning well over two years before the Erie-Lackawanna merger of October 17, 1960, two-tone green Erie 820 departs Dearborn with Number 6, *The Lake Cities*.

Right . . . A decade later, on a bitter January 1968 morning, E8A 814 starts a five-car *Lake Cities* toward New York.

Above . . . The fourteen ex-Erie Railroad PA's were not common sights on EL varnish after the early 1960's. Primarily assigned to freight duty by 1967, two of the renowned Alco's, 857 and 863, will get a high-speed workout with #6 on a frigid February 25th.

Upper right . . . Erie Lackawanna 814, EMD class of 1951, pauses on the leads to Dearborn as Santa Fe 2396 works the depot. The Alco RS1 predates the E8 by some four years having been built in 1947, and on this September 6, 1965 is serving as a Dearborn switcher.

Lower right . . . At State Line Tower in Hammond, EL's six-car eastbound *Lake Cities* has just entered Indiana with E8A 824 on the point. The date is a cold and windy January 19, 1965. Erie Lackawanna's 809-819 were ex-Delaware, Lackawanna & Western 820, 810-819. EL 820-833 were ex-Erie units of the same numbers. All twenty-five of the E8A's were constructed in 1951. For a short time Number 6 was renamed *The World's Fair* because of the New York World's Fair of 1964-65.

Above . . . B&O's *Washington Express* leaves Chicago's Grand Central Station in May 1965 with E7A 1424 leading the way.

Below . . . E7A 1419 is about to duck under the Roosevelt Road (12th Street) overpass with another Number 10, the *Chicago-Washington Express* in April 1962.

Right . . . Premier train on the Chicago-Washington run was the Baltimore & Ohio's *Capitol Limited.* The East's first domes and this distinctive obs highlighted the handsome consist. At 4:10 PM on June 7, 1964, blue and gray EMD 1438 and mates are twenty minutes away from urging the *Capitol* out of Chicago's Grand Central.

Above . . . In the decade preceding Amtrak, Chesapeake & Ohio's passenger business out of the Windy City was confined to the Chicago-Grand Rapids (Michigan) route. E7 4521 powers #10, ready to depart Grand Central on March 27, 1964.

Upper right . . . On a delightful May 1964 afternoon, Chessie's train #8 awaits departure time in Chicago. Although not individually named, C&O's Chicago trains carried a collective label of *The Pere Marquettes*. The mostly-in-Michigan Pere Marquette was merged into the Chesapeake & Ohio on June 6, 1947.

Lower right . . . Not listed in the timetables, a special train departs Grand Central behind the 4510 on April 20, 1962.

Upper right . . . In 1956 the passenger service of Canadian National-subsidiary Grand Trunk Western was entirely in the hands of handsome 4-8-4's out of Chicago (both steam and diesel were working freight). Alco-built U3b 6334 rides the turntable at the GTW's Elsdon Yard in September 1956 after bringing #15, the *International Limited*, in from Michigan.

Above . . . The day is drab and cold as the 6408 thunders out of the curve past Elsdon Yard and across 55th Street in Chicago. It is February 5, 1957—the last week for GTW steam in Chicago (although steam-powered runs continued for three more years in the Detroit area). Lima built U4b's 6405-6410 in 1938 with a streamlined jacket similar to the CN's own 6400-6404. The train is Number 20, the *Maple Leaf*.

Lower right . . . Pairs of EMD Geeps, operated long hood forward, replaced steam on the Grand Trunk's passenger trains. On August 16, 1964, Geeps 4952 and 4913 curve under Clark Street with #20.

Above . . . A fresh snow blankets Chicago on Christmas morning in 1965. Grand Trunk's inbound *International* approaches 18th Street, a mile or so out of Dearborn, behind long-nosed Geeps 4930 and 4900.

Upper right . . . CN Pullmans congregate at Chicago's Dearborn in May 1964.

Lower right . . . Three, instead of the usual two, Grand Trunk Western motors pull the *Maple Leaf* away from Dearborn in April 1962. First and third units, 4930 and 4137 are 1958-built GP9's, while two year old GP18 4951 holds down the middle slot in the lash-up.

Left . . . Flagship train of the Delaware, Lackawanna & Western was its New York-Buffalo (actually Hoboken-Buffalo) *Phoebe Snow* inaugurated November 15, 1949. *Phoebe* began visiting Chicago following the E-L merger when, in September 1963, the *Erie-Lackawanna Limited* was renamed the *Phoebe Snow*. EMD 828 awaits the late afternoon departure time for the *Phoebe Snow* on October 2, 1966. Eight weeks later, on Sunday, November 27, 1966, *Phoebe* left Chicago for the last time.

Below . . . A pair of Electro-Motive's graceful E's swing the Dearborn-bound *Lake Cities* past the 47th Street depot in April 1969.

Above and below . . . On a hazy, "brisk", ten above zero morning, EL's *Lake Cities* rolls out of Dearborn Station for the last time, ending Erie-Lackawanna passenger service to Chicago. Powering #6 on this January 4, 1970 are ex-Erie E8A's 825 and 829.

The Nickel Plate, officially the New York, Chicago & St. Louis Railroad Company, concentrated on its freight business, content to let giant neighbor New York Central worry over passengers. Nevertheless the NKP did manage a comfortable service and in diesels opted for Alco's classic PA's.

Left . . . Two of the blue and white Alco's accelerate out of La Salle Station in May 1961, bound for Buffalo with #8, *The New Yorker*. (Service continued beyond Buffalo to New York via the Erie-Lackawanna.)

Above . . . "Bluebird" 186 teams with Geep 479 to move Number 8 by 16th Street in April 1962, the last year for the PA's on the Nickel Plate.

Below . . . During 1962 ten Alco RS36's replaced the Nickel Plate's ten PA's. Nearing 16th Street, Alco 874 and EMD 481 bring the inbound *City of Chicago* toward La Salle Street. Strangely enough, in spite of Chicago's reputation as the rail capital of the U.S., there was no *City of Chicago* in the Union Pacific's *Cities* fleet, no *Chicago Zephyr* in the Burlington fleet, no *Chicago Chief* on the Santa Fe (the AT&SF did timetable a *Chicagoan*), no *Chicago "400"*, and so forth.

Grand Central was, in the author's opinion, the most deserving of Chicago's rail stations to receive historical landmark status and preservation. Unfortunately it also was the first of Chicago's six major stations to be dismantled. Opened in December 1890, Grand Central began hosting Baltimore & Ohio trains in late 1891 and Chesapeake & Ohio trains in 1903. Both roads stayed at Grand Central until the station was closed after the departures of November 8, 1969. The Chicago Great Western was a long time occupant until the end of its Chicago passenger service in 1956. Grand Central also was home for the Wisconsin Central (Soo Line) for many years until the Soo moved its last remaining pair of trains, the Chicago-Superior/Duluth *Lakers,* to the Illinois Central Station in 1963.

B&O's blue 1955-built E9A 1456 idles under Grand Central's huge shed after bringing in #7, the *Diplomat*, in July 1966. After Grand Central closed in 1969, B&O/C&O trains moved to North Western Station until they were discontinued with the coming of Amtrak in 1971.

Above . . . With 1449 on the point, the *Capitol Limited* is off and running on its way to Washington in May 1964. *Capitol Limited* service began on May 13, 1923 and ended with the departure (from C&NW Station) on April 30, 1971.

Below . . . EMD's 1444 and 1410 haul the *Washington Express* out of Grand Central and under Chicago's favorite passenger train-watching location—the Roosevelt Road overpass. In the distance B&O 3540 is working as the depot switcher on this August morning in 1966.

Above . . . A mile out of Grand Central, B&O's 1434 is swinging into the ascending curve which will take it across the bridge over the South Branch of the Chicago River. The date is November 3, 1963.

Below . . . On this May 31st, 1964, B&O's Number 10 departed Grand Central as scheduled all right. Nearly one hour later however, E's 1454 and 1408 are wheeling #10 south on the New York Central/Rock Island route out of La Salle toward Englewood, just south of the Illinois Central crossing at 16th Street. Apparently track work, or possibly a derailment on the regular routing, resulted in the irregular operation.

Above . . . Chesapeake & Ohio train 8 awaits its Chicago departure time in 1964. Grand Central's huge semicircular train shed spanned six tracks, but during the time frame of this book was rarely crowded. C&O 4514, ex-Pere Marquette 107, is assigned to #8 today. B&O's *Capitol* already has departed and after 4514 leaves for Michigan, Grand Central will be quiet for several hours.

Left and right . . . Electro-Motive built a small fleet of thirty-one E8A's for the Chesapeake & Ohio with road numbers 4000-4030. Thirteen and a half years into a service life which was to span two decades, 4003 idles in a glistening light rain during February 1965. A year later sister 4004 waits with another train 8 at Grand Central.

Above . . . During the 1960's a bold, white GT on a black background was replacing the smaller, more elegant lettering on previously olive green/yellow Grand Trunk Western Geeps. On September 1, 1965 the 4908 sweeps past 18th Street with the Canada-bound *Maple Leaf.*

Below . . . Toronto-Chicago passenger service acquired an even more distinct Canadian flavor in the late 1960's. Canadian National F's were assigned as power all the way to Dearborn, replacing GTW Geeps on the Grand Trunk portion of the run. Here 6535 is leading an A-B-A set of CN wagons bringing #158, the *Maple Leaf,* out of Dearborn Station near 18th Street in February 1969.

Above . . . Train 158 rounds the curve approaching 47th Street with FP9A's 6533 and 6540 providing the horsepower. Freshly painted Erie Lackawanna RS3 1031 observes the action from the adjacent yard. The 1952-built Alco has six years seniority on the FP's.

Below . . . Ten miles out of Dearborn Station, the April 20th, 1969 version of the Toronto-bound *Maple Leaf* brakes for the Chicago Lawn stop on the Grand Trunk Western. These classy GTW/CN trains were one of the few bright spots in an otherwise rather bleak passenger train picture east out of Chicago in the last year or two before Amtrak arrived on the scene.

Upper left . . . In early 1956, Electro-Motive produced three locomotives for use with lightweight passenger equipment. Each of the 1200 horsepower units utilized a prime mover of the same type found in EMD's E9 (the E9's each had two of the 567C engines of course). One of the two EMD Aerotrain demonstrator sets (locomotive 1001) was leased to the New York Central during the summer of 1956. On September 9th the westbound Aerotrain, operating Cleveland to Chicago, pauses at Englewood Union Station (63rd Street). All three train sets were sold to the Rock Island where they wound up working Chicago commuter schedules until their short careers ended in 1965.

Lower left . . . Elegance on wheels! The Central's *Twentieth Century Limiteds*, along with Santa Fe's *Super Chief*, were no doubt America's most well-known luxury trains. Here, Englewood's depot is rapidly disappearing in the wake of an already flying Gotham-bound *Century*. Two-tone gray Observation-Lounge cars *Hickory Creek* and *Sandy Creek* were built by Pullman-Standard in 1949 for the *Century*.

Above . . . Clad in the classic "lightning stripe" gray and white dress, New York Central E's pass on the leads to La Salle Street Station in 1962. Outbound 4078 is working #356, the *Twilight Limited*, while the 4058 waits for the action to subside. La Salle was completed in 1903 and became the Chicago terminal for the Rock Island and the Nickel Plate, as well as the New York Central.

Above . . . Budd-built Coach 2920, in the consist of one of the lesser trains of "The Great Steel Fleet", pauses at Englewood.

Below . . . E8A 4076 strides into Englewood in June 1966 with #28, the *New England States*.

Right . . . Stainless steel Observation-Parlor cars occasionally replaced *Sandy Creek* and *Hickory Creek* on the *Century* when the regular cars were being shopped.

Above . . . Near 16th Street, Central E7A 4011 is backlit by the afternoon sun. The EMD is due for an assignment on the point of one of the NYC express/mail trains.

Upper right . . . Competitors meet at Englewood! Although Pennsy's *Broadway Limited* and Central's *Twentieth Century* were scheduled inbound into Englewood at nearly the same time over the years, it wasn't all that often that both were briefly motionless on adjacent rails for photographs.

Lower right . . . An era ends on October 26, 1968. The glory years are over, the *Century* runs no more and even the proud New York Central is now part of the Penn Central, as 4081 heads the last Central train to depart from La Salle Street Station (PC #366). Tomorrow all remaining Penn Central trains will depart over Pennsy's Union Station rails.

Upper left . . . Ninety-six E-type cabs handled most New York Central passenger trains (thirty-six E7A's and sixty E8A's). In July 1966 the 4080 waits to depart Englewood with the Chicago-bound *New England States*. Rock Island's *Peoria Rocket*, with E8A 646 built two years earlier than the 4080, vies for the first to be off for La Salle Street.

Lower left . . . New York Central's finest, the *Twentieth Century Limited*, is underway out of Englewood at a rapidly increasing pace behind three all-out E's. To the right, Pennsylvania's *General* has not yet gotten the highball, but the pace will be just as swift once it comes.

Top . . . The *Century* loads at Englewood behind the 4075 as Pennsy's *General* arrives with 4302 as the lead unit.

Lower . . . Another meet at Englewood finds EMD 4054 bringing *The Chicagoan* into town as sister 4056 briefly idles while passengers board the *Century* for New York. Both 1952-built units eventually were to work for Amtrak. The *Century*, which began operating on June 15, 1902, left Chicago for the last time on December 2, 1967.

Pennsy's finest was the all-Pullman Chicago-New York *Broadway Limited*. Urged east in steam days by double-headed K4s Pacifics and later by a Loewy-streamlined 4-4-4-4 duplex, the dieselized *Broadway* was led by Tuscan red E's, elegantly pin-striped in gold.

Above . . . A-B-A E7's back the Pullmans into Union Station in 1962, shortly before the *Broadway's* late afternoon departure time. EMD 5863 still carries the tasteful gold pin-striping, but most units now were getting a simplified single broad stripe. Chicago's Union Station was the newest of the six major rail stations with a completion date of 1925. Calling Union Station home, in addition to the Pennsylvania Railroad, were the Burlington Route, the Milwaukee Road and the Chicago & Alton (later the Gulf, Mobile & Ohio). Competition was keener at Union than at any other of Chicago's downtown depots. Both the Q and the MILW served up great trains to the Twin Cities, the Pacific Northwest and San Francisco, departing from the same station (although from opposite sides).

Left . . . The morning sun welcomes the inbound *Broadway* as it makes a brief stop at Englewood.

Upper left . . . The Red Team's 4269 cruises into Englewood with train 55, the *Pennsylvania Limited*. (New York Central was the Green Team.) GP35 2295, heading a westbound freight, waits to follow the varnish north as far as the 59th St. yard. Prior to the anticipated Penn Central merger, Pennsy E's were renumbered to mesh with New York Central's numbers. PRR 4269 is ex-5769 and would go on to Amtrak in the 1970's as their 279.

Lower left . . . *Tower View* gets an unscheduled washing as the eastbound *Broadway* stops at Englewood in the midst of a June thunderstorm. Two of these observation cars, *Tower View* and *Mountain View*, were built for *Broadway Limited* duty by Pullman-Standard in 1949, the same year P-S built two obs cars for New York Central's *Century*.

Below . . . Englewood was a very busy spot in the great days of the passenger train. But as the 1960's wore on, the crowds thinned out and quiet moments came more often. Although a few trains continued to stop at Englewood for a while longer, the last day the familiar station was open for business was April 9, 1969.

Above . . . On this June morning the inbound *Broadway*, behind the 5805, is running one hour late as it meets a departing *South Wind* just out of Englewood. Despite the disparity in numbers, PRR 5805 and the 4249, leading the *South Wind*, are close cousins. Both E8's were built at La Grange in mid-1952 (railroad class EP22). The 4249 was originally the 5789 and the 5805 will soon become 4270.

Upper right . . . 4281 urges the *General* out of Englewood in September 1966.

Lower right . . . At 12:13 PM three of Pennsy's Tuscan red E8's haul a lengthy *Manhattan Limited* away from the Gary, Indiana depot. The date is September 23, 1965.

Left . . . Framed by the bracing for the signal bridge seen in the photograph at the lower right, the eastbound *Broadway* departs Englewood.

Below . . . Under leaden skies threatening more snow, the Pennsylvania Railroad's 5761 clatters across the Chicago, South Shore & South Bend's electrified trackage in Burnham, Illinois. Trailing the E8A is PRR #70, a Chicago-Cincinnati schedule.

Upper right . . . It looks like the painters had a bad day when PRR 4266 came through the shop in 1966. Now let's see, where can we put that "P"?

Lower right . . . Ex-5709, now the 4279, brings eastbound train 22, the *Manhattan Limited*, into Englewood in February 1967, one year before the Penn Central merger. Sticking with steam power for passenger duty through the early diesel years, neither the Pennsylvania nor rival New York Central bought slant-nosed E's. Both started with E7A's and E7B's, then purchased large fleets of E8A's (but no E8B's) and neither opted for E9's, a rather striking similarity. (Both dabbled in PA's and FM's, the most noticeable difference was the Pennsy order for the big Baldwin Sharks and Centipedes.) The Pennsylvania schedule to the East changed very little from 1960 until the PC merger of early 1968. There was the morning *Manhattan Limited*, the afternoon *General* and *Broadway*, and finally the evening departures of *The Admiral* and the combined *Pennsylvania Limited/Golden Triangle*.

The Wabash was one of those railroads which was difficult to categorize. Was it an Eastern road? After all the Wabash rolled east to Fort Wayne, Toledo and Detroit, well into Pennsy territory, and its freight trains reached the Buffalo area. Or was it a Midwestern railroad? Wabash trains headed west to Omaha and Kansas City and, in conjunction with the Union Pacific, its *City of St. Louis* reached L.A. The October 1964 merger solved the problem by putting the leased Wabash, along with the merged Nickel Plate, into the Norfolk & Western camp.

Above . . . Out of Chicago the Wabash scheduled the morning *Banner Blue* and the afternoon *Blue Bird* to St. Louis. Competition on this route came from the Illinois Central, the Gulf, Mobile & Ohio, and to a lesser extent, from the C&EI. EMD 1003 departs Dearborn Station in June 1958 with #11, the *Banner Blue*. E8A's 1003-1015 (railroad class D-22) came from Electro-Motive between 1949 and 1953.

Lower right . . . The outbound *Blue Bird* rounds the curve at 21st Street behind the 1005 and Alco PA 1053 on August 25, 1964.

Upper right . . . In April 1966 ex-Wabash 1015, now Norfolk & Western 3815, leads the Chicago-St. Louis *Banner Blue* at 18th Street.

Above . . . Wabash 1017, renumbered from 1002A, leaves Dearborn's trainshed with the *Banner Blue* in September 1965. In another nineteen minutes Santa Fe's 303 will be underway for Kansas City and California with the *Grand Canyon.*

Upper left . . . E8A's 1003 and 1006 approach 18th Street with #11 in October 1964.

Lower left . . . Norfolk & Western 3815 ducks under Clark Street in June 1966. The N&W did not purchase any cabtype units on its own, but acquired both E's and F's when it absorbed the Wabash. Only a handful of the Wabash E's were renumbered to N&W before being scrapped or traded in on new freight power.

Above . . . The every-other-day Chicago to Florida *South Wind* drew power alternately from two of its participating carriers, the Pennsylvania Railroad and the Atlantic Coast Line. The days of purple paint are long gone as a team of ACL's black E's accelerates #90 out of Union Station in May 1966. *South Wind* competition for the Florida trade came from the Illinois Central-Central of Georgia *City of Miami* and from the C&EI.

Upper right . . . North of Evansville, Indiana, trains from such diverse areas of the South as Florida, Atlanta and New Orleans were funneled to Chicago on the rails of the Chicago & Eastern Illinois. In September 1956, blue and orange 1604 bounds into the 63rd Street Englewood stop with *The Humming Bird* from New Orleans via Mobile, Montgomery and Nashville.

Lower right . . . A trio of Louisville & Nashville E's, 759, 773 and 796, powers the combined *Georgian/Humming Bird* departing Chicago in July 1966. From the front the yellow-nosed E7 on the point carries no identifying markings as to its owner.

Left . . . On October 17, 1964, one day after the Wabash was absorbed into the Norfolk & Western, the *Banner Blue* exits Dearborn behind Wabash's E8A 1003.

Above . . . By this July 1958 date the C&EI's ten 1600-series passenger FP7's were receiving a simplified, and much more solemn, dark blue dress. The class engine stands ready to depart the Windy City with the *Georgian/Humming Bird*.

Above . . . Gulf, Mobile & Ohio's red and maroon 101 pokes its impressive and racy length out of the shadow of the Polk Street overpass departing Union Station with #1 in August 1963.

Right . . . *The Limited*, train 1, races through Dwight, Illinois, passing signals with a distinct B&O flavor. The eastern carrier controlled GM&O's Illinois predecessor, Chicago & Alton, in the 1930's and early 40's. GM&O's red and maroon colors also were inherited from the Alton Route.

Left . . . Train #1, known only as *The Limited* by the 1960's (but at one time *The Alton Limited)*, charges through Lorenzo, Illinois on January 25, 1968. To the right of the speeding 102A, a Santa Fe local is in the hole on the joint GM&O/AT&SF trackage. The use of two single tracks to form a joint double-track extends approximately 16 miles from the outskirts of Joliet, at Plaines, to Pequot, approaching Coal City.

Above and below . . . EMD 103A opens up after rolling through the GM&O's junction at Mazonia, where the two separate routes to Joliet (and Chicago) diverge. The northbound *Abraham Lincoln* will operate via the Pequot route. Heavyweight diner 1076 originally was built for the Chicago & Alton's *Alton Limited.*

Left . . . On July 24, 1966, EMD power pulls *The Limited* around the curve at 21st Street. GM&O's E7A's 100-103 and 101A-103A worked the Chicago-St. Louis run for nearly three decades, first for the Alton, then the GM&O and finally for Amtrak in the early 1970's. Unit 100A was an E8A built in 1953 for a traded-in 1937 Baltimore & Ohio EA.

Above . . . In addition to the Gulf, Mobile & Ohio's small stable of E's, several F3's were available for passenger duty and to work its single Chicago-Joliet commuter run. On May 10, 1968, 885A draws the lead assignment on the GM&O's top train, the *Abraham Lincoln*, shown here speeding through suburban Willow Springs.

Below . . . In full flight, 101 and mate are about to beat a rapid cadence of steel on steel at the Penn Central's Kankakee Belt diamond as they approach Dwight, Illinois with Number 1. The date is August 29, 1970.

Above . . . Five of the slant-nosed E6A's built by EMD in 1940 and 1941 hauled passengers for the Illinois Central. On August 17, 1964 the 4003 was the lead unit in charge of #14, the *Land O'Corn*, as it docked in the IC's Central Station. Central was built for the Columbian Exposition of 1893 and in addition to being home for all of IC's intercity trains, Central hosted Michigan Central and Big Four passenger trains (instead of La Salle) under a long-term lease. In addition the Soo's *Laker* worked out of Central from 1963 until it was discontinued in January 1965.

Upper right . . . The *Land O'Corn* rolls past the Santa Fe's 18th Street passenger facilities in June 1965, enroute across northern Illinois to Dubuque and Waterloo, Iowa. E9A 4035, new in 1954, carries the IC's delightful colors of orange and chocolate trimmed with yellow.

Lower right . . . Number 14, the inbound *'Corn* charges into suburban Broadview, about thirty minutes out of Central Station. The red IC caboose trails an eastbound freight waiting to follow the 4004 east in June 1962.

Below . . . Chicago & Eastern Illinois F's 1606 and 1604 are moments away from a late afternoon departure from Dearborn Station with the combined *Georgian/Humming Bird* in May 1965.

Upper left . . . On a foggy February 1, 1968, Number 93 prepares to leave Dearborn for the last time. After the *Georgian/Humming Bird* leaves C&EI rails, the carrier's passenger business will be reduced to a Chicago-Danville, Illinois local.

Lower left . . . C&EI 28, formerly the 1101, zips by 47th Street with the "Danville Flyer" in July 1968. The Illinois road purchased E7A's 1100-1102 in 1946 but thereafter switched to F's instead of E8's. Unit 1102 was wrecked in 1958 and was traded in for an E9A of the same number.

Above . . . The Fourth of July 1959 finds Monon's F3A 84A departing Dearborn with the five-car *Thoroughbred*, bound for Louisville. Trackage of the little (547 route miles) Monon lay entirely in the Hoosier State of Indiana except for the terminal cities of Chicago and Louisville.

Upper right . . . Monon's #11, *The Tippecanoe*, pulls into Chicago's "other" Englewood behind red, gray and white 84B in September 1956. The 63rd Street stop for trains of the Monon, Erie and C&EI, plus Chicago & Western Indiana suburban service, was not nearly as well known (or as busy) as its NYC/PRR/CRI&P/NKP neighbor further east.

Below . . . Colors for the Monon's freight diesels were black and gold, modeled here by F3A 85B on this July 1958 afternoon. In the late 1950's and early 1960's Monon passenger locomotives and rolling stock lost their familiar red and gray and received the freight scheme. The Monon, at one time the Chicago, Indianapolis & Louisville after its main terminals, received its shortened name from the small Indiana town where the Chicago-Indianapolis line crossed the Michigan City-Louisville line.

Opposite page, top . . . Monon 83A and 81A pull #5 to a brief stop at 63rd Street in November 1956. EMD built F3A's 81A,B through 84A,B in 1947.

Opposite page, bottom . . . Ex-82B, now the 204 in gold and black, is just south of 47th Street with a five-car #5, the *Thoroughbred*, in May 1966.

Left . . . In July 1958 the 81B carries the Hoosier Line slogan of the Monon.

Below . . . In the last year of Monon's small passenger business, high-nosed Alco Century 420's 501 and 502 took over for the twenty year old F's. At 6:06 PM on August 20, 1967, the 502 stops in Hammond, Indiana with #5. One month later, on September 29, 1967, the last Number 5 left Chicago and the Monon became freight only.

Above . . . Illinois Central's 1946-built 4009 idles in Broadview on the point of Number 13. Momentarily the E7A will be off toward Iowa in the gathering darkness of this October 1964 evening.

Below . . . Last survivors of the IC E6A's were the 4001 and 4003. A late March snow covers the ground as one of the venerable EMD's, 4003, accelerates what is left of the *Green Diamond* service toward St. Louis in 1965.

Above . . . A more modernistic IC emblem has replaced the traditional green herald on the nose of E9 4040. EMD 4040 and Central of Georgia 812 are working the inbound *Seminole* at south suburban Homewood in April 1968.

Below . . . Pride of the "Main Line of Mid-America" was the overnight Chicago-New Orleans *Panama Limited*. At dusk a March 1970 version of the *Panama* roars south near Monee, Illinois behind a trio of E's led by the 4042. *Panama Limited* service began in 1911.

Above . . . Well it's one of those days in Chicago! E7A 4017 carries a generous crusting of ice as it gathers its breath for the last lap from Broadview into Chicago with train 14. Frequently a recipient of snow and cold in the winter months, Chicago normally does not get many ice storms, but this January 23rd, 1965, is a well-remembered exception.

Upper right . . . Pinch-hitting for E's, a pair of black GP9's, 9202 and 9201, hustles the outbound *Land O'Corn* around a curve a mile or so west of the busy 21st Street diamonds. Steam generator equipped 9200-9203 appeared at frequent intervals on the IC's Iowa trains in the 1960's.

Lower right . . . Business Car 5 (or Office Car, as the plate on the door reads) spends a quiet February 1966 afternoon on a siding at Central Station.

If there was one constant over the quarter century covered in this volume, it was the passenger service of the Chicago, South Shore & South Bend. It was not that the CSS&SB wanted it so, for all the equipment was built in the 1920's. But passenger deficits kept the South Shore from accumulating capital (and from getting financing) for new coaches. So the South Shore of 1981 was much unchanged, except for advancing age, from the CSS&SB of 1956. Change is coming though and 1983 should see a complete re-equipping of South Shore trains, and the retirement of the familiar orange interurban-style cars.

Above . . . Coach 38 swings through the curve at 130th Street in far south Chicago with a three-car train in January 1965. In about two miles the trio will move onto the Illinois Central's electrified trackage at Kensington for the dash downtown.

Upper right . . . Three-car Saturday/Sunday/Holiday train 319 passes South Shore's freight motors 701-702 working near Clark Road in Gary, Indiana. Rebuilt combine 109 heads the parade in 1964. Motors 701-707 were ex-New York Central electrics acquired in the mid-1950's, rebuilt by the South Shore, and eventually retired in the mid-1970's.

Lower right . . . A few feet east of the Illinois/Indiana state line, coach 21 leads CSS&SB train 523 into Hammond on a gloomy November 21, 1970.

The electrified Chicago, North Shore & Milwaukee operated fast and frequent service along the west side of Lake Michigan in the area indicated by its corporate title.

Above . . . Two sets of *Electroliner* equipment regularly spun off the 87 miles between Chicago and Milwaukee in one hour and fifty minutes including stops and some slow-speed street running in Milwaukee. *Electroliners* 801-802 and 803-804 came from the St. Louis Car Company and went into service during February 1941. In its last winter of operation for the North Shore the 801-802 set sweeps through the curve at Lake Bluff, Illinois with train 802. Both *Electroliners* were sold to the Philadelphia Suburban Transportation Company in September 1963 where they were renamed *Liberty Liners*.

Upper left . . . An extra operated for sailors from the Great Lakes Naval Training Center speeds through Lake Bluff on a bitter January 20, 1963. Lead coach 725 was built in 1926.

Lower left . . . A somewhat more leisurely branch extended from the North Shore main west to Libertyville and Mundelein. Coach 175, built in 1920, leads a two-car train drifting up to the Mundelein depot, ready to work an early afternoon departure. Lack of capital for a massive replacement of its elderly rolling stock, and a declining business, led to the cessation of North Shore service early on the morning of January 21, 1963.

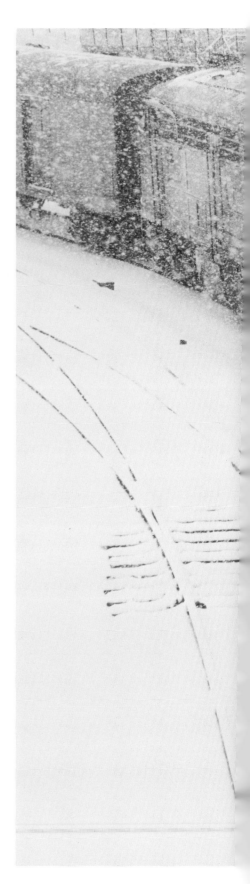

Above . . . Engine 29C idles on a misty Chicago evening as the passengers board Santa Fe's *Texas Chief* (#15) in early 1965. The *Texas Chief* would continue on into the Amtrak days and eventually be renamed *The Lone Star.*

Right . . . Mother Nature has a special touch for those cities around the five Great Lakes. In addition to getting snows from passing storms, whenever winter winds blow off the relatively "warmer" waters of the Lakes, more snow falls—up to two inches per hour until the wind changes and somebody else catches it. Santa Fe PA's 67 and 74 loom out of a Lake Michigan snow squall with #23 at Clark St. on January 6, 1968. Trains 23/24, the *Grand Canyon Limiteds,* regularly ran in two or three sections behind steam into the early 1950's. As the number of passenger trains decreased on the AT&SF in later years, the economy-style *Canyon* gradually became the all-stops workhorse from Chicago to California.

Above . . . In a moment the headlight will flick on. Santa Fe 46 and its four companions will ease into motion and #9, the *Kansas City Chief*, will be underway toward its namesake city. On this March 1964 date, six departures from Dearborn still were listed in the Santa Fe timetables.

Upper right . . . Business Car 32 adds a touch of class to #23 departing Chicago. It is May 1965 and the *Grand Canyon* has become the Santa Fe's "local" to California. Up front the F's on the point are approaching the 21st Street diamonds.

Lower right . . . Santa Fe's #16, the inbound *Texas Chief*, sweeps past the GE's waiting to bring an eastbound Illinois Central freight across the 21st St. crossing. Electro-Motive assembled F7A number 45 for the AT&SF in 1952, while IC's 5004, on the inbound from Iowa, came from General Electric in 1967.

Above . . . Santa Fe PA's 74 and 67 work #24 through Lemont, Illinois at 2:22 PM on January 16, 1968. In a last fling at main line glory, the handsome Alco's worked 23 and 24 for about six weeks during the winter of 1967-68.

Right . . . Pride of the Santa Fe's fleet of luxury trains was the extra fare, all-Pullman *Super Chief*. Numbers 17 and 18 ran off the 2222 Chicago-Los Angeles miles in just under forty hours. The first *Super Chief* (with standard cars) began once-a-week service on May 12, 1936. A year later, on May 18th, stainless steel equipment took over on the *Super*. Daily departures began on February 29, 1948 and the train was re-equipped in 1951. The *Super's* dome is silhouetted against a darkening sky in Joliet, *top*. By the mid-1960's the *Super Chief* often was combined with the *El Capitan* as at Dearborn in 1964 (round-end obs were withdrawn in 1958). In 1967 the AT&SF purchased nine 3600 horsepower FP45's to replace the F's on the *Super Chief*. Renumbered from 105, the 5945 roars east with #18 near Lorenzo, Illinois in March 1971.

Above . . . Joliet was the last stop before Dearborn for Santa Fe's Chicago-bound trains. On October 28, 1966, the *San Francisco Chief* is poised for the last lap from the Pacific coast to the shores of Lake Michigan. Hi-level Coach 702 was part of a twenty-five car order constructed by the Budd Company in 1956.

Upper right . . . Typical of the very small Midwestern hamlet, Lorenzo has the railroad, a general store, an elevator and a handful of houses. 40C has the westbound *San Francisco Chief*, train #1, in tow on February 1, 1969.

Lower right . . . New Year's Day 1967 finds Santa Fe's only E3 cab leading Second 19, the second section of the *Chief*, at Clark Street. Built in 1939, the 11 would serve the Santa Fe until June 1968, a pretty good career for one of those newfangled "Diesels" which wasn't supposed to last in strenuous railroad duty.

Above . . . Santa Fe's *Texas Chief,* nearing the end of its journey from the Lone Star State, pulls away from a Joliet stop in late April 1971. Rock Island's yellow and maroon 650, just in from Peoria, also is bound for Chicago. Amtrak is a week away from becoming a reality; Santa Fe will turn its passenger trains over to the new corporation but the Rock Island will not.

Upper right . . . Five years earlier, on an April morning in 1966, the same 650 works the same inbound train from Peoria.

Lower right . . . The scene is Englewood in August 1966. On the right 677 is shoving a Chicago area push-pull suburban train into the station. Meanwhile E8A 643 is just underway with Rock Island's westbound *Rocky Mountain Rocket.* The 643 was Electro-Motive's first E8, demonstrator 952 built in 1949 and acquired by the Rock Island in 1950. Competing with Burlington's *Denver Zephyr* and Union Pacific's *City of Denver,* the *Rocky Mountain Rocket* operated via Des Moines, Omaha and Lincoln to Denver and Colorado Springs.

Upper left . . . Rock Island's *Golden State* was the road's luxury schedule to California. Alco DL109 621, repowered with an Electro-Motive prime mover in 1953, heads No. 3 at Joliet in September 1966. West of Tucumcari, New Mexico the *Golden State* will be forwarded by the Southern Pacific.

Above . . . A more commonplace unit is on the point of the outbound *Golden State* just south of the 16th St. crossing of the Illinois Central's Iowa line. E7A 632 was the first of eleven cabs (632-642) built by EMD for the Rock Island between 1946 and 1948. The *Golden State Limited* was introduced in November 1902 (the same year as New York Central's *Twentieth Century*); the last Chicago arrival for the *Golden State* pulled into La Salle on February 21, 1968 (just a few months after the last run of the *Century*).

Lower left . . . Coach 342, the *Golden Trumpet*, built by Pullman-Standard in 1947 for the *Golden State*, lasted until the curtain came down on Rock Island intercity passenger service at the end of 1978. In 1968 the 342 was in the consist of No. 6 from Rock Island as it pulled into Englewood.

Above . . . Rock Island crews exchange greetings at Englewood on June 25, 1966. On the right FP7A 408 leads the *Des Moines Rocket* outbound. E7 638 waits for Number 5 to leave before pulling to a stop at the depot with #14 from Peoria.

Upper right . . . Citing an inability to pay the required entrance fee, the Rock Island did not join Amtrak in 1971 and therefore was obliged to continue operation of its existing trains (Chicago-Peoria #11/12 and Chicago-Rock Island #5/6). Number 5's short but still classy consist curved by the New Lenox depot in August 1974 behind E8A 652.

Lower right . . . By July 1977 the lack of passengers (and funds) was acute and the little trains were taking on a rather forlorn appearance, but they would continue to run until the end of December 1978. 655 leads and 1948-built Budd Coach *Herington* trails at Joliet.

When the Burlington inaugurated its first streamlined stainless steel *Zephyr* in 1934, it quickly earned a reputation where *Zephyr* was synonymous with speed that lasted right up to Amtrak. And deservedly so! Over the years various portions of CB&Q passenger runs ranked right at or near the top in speed surveys.

Above . . . One of the Q's silver E5's leads a lesser known train, the overnight *American Royal Zephyr* and the *Ak-Sar-Ben Zephyr*, combined east of Galesburg, past the Burlington's Chicago coach yard in April 1962. A mix of old and new suburban equipment dots the yard in the midst of the morning rush hour.

Upper left . . . Traces of winter still linger on this mid-March afternoon as the eastbound *North Coast Limited* speeds through Shabbona, Illinois, 67 miles out of Union Station. Pride of the "Main Street of the Northwest", Northern Pacific/Burlington's two-tone green domeliner received its distinctive styling from Raymond Loewy in 1952. Observation Car 392 was one of five built by Pullman-Standard in mid-1948 for the NP. Prior to 1954, obs 392 was named *Tacoma Club*.

Lower left . . . Burlington's #1 was the sleek and speedy westbound *Denver Zephyr*. In contrast #2 was the morning all-stops-across Illinois "Galesburg Local". (The eastbound *Denver Zephyr* was #10.) Trailing E5 9915A and a Pullman-green coach on an April 1962 #2 is the "*Silver Pendulum*". Coach 6000 was an experimental car built in 1940 by the Pacific Railway Equipment Company. (Shortly before the BN merger the eastbound *DZ* was renumbered to #2.)

Above . . . Four silver Burlington E's led by the 9975 race west beyond Sugar Grove with combined #31/25. Vast corn fields line the right-of-way through the Illinois prairie. It is mid-September 1969 and the Q's schedules to the Pacific Northwest normally are combined between Chicago and the Twin Cities in off-peak periods.

Upper right . . . Coffee Shop Diner Lounge *Iceberg Lake* is in the consist of the *Empire Builder* making a passenger stop in Aurora. American Car & Foundry built the 1243 in 1951.

Lower right . . . America's favorite land cruise in the 1950's and 1960's was the *California Zephyr*. Traversing the Rockies and the Feather River Canyon during daylight hours (in both directions) was a treat unequalled in standard gauge railroading. Here the *CZ* rambles west three miles beyond Earlville, Illinois, on February 21, 1970 with Q 9932B on the point. *California Zephyr* service began on March 20, 1949 and the final departure left Chicago on March 20, 1970 with CB&Q 9965 leading.

Above . . . Beginning in October 1955, the Union Pacific's West Coast trains began operating over Milwaukee rails east of the Missouri River. Thirteen years later, on October 21, 1968, the domeliner *City of San Francisco/City of Los Angeles* (combined) departs Davis Jct., Illinois on the last lap of its journey to Chicago. The three E's up front have #102/104 on time.

Upper left . . . It was the practice of some of Chicago's railroads to back the entire train, power and all, from a nearby coach yard into the downtown station. That is the scene on this August 1966 evening as UP 903 shoves the *City of Los Angeles* into Union Station. Coming up on the right is Milwaukee's No. 11, the *Sioux*, bound for Madison, Wisconsin behind E7A 17B.

Lower left . . . The February 26, 1967 version of Milwaukee's *Morning Hiawatha* moves out of the depths of Union Station into the cold winter sunshine. Initial *Hiawatha* service inaugurated in May 1935 became the *Afternoon Hiawatha* when a second train, the *Morning Hiawatha*, was added in January 1939. Lead unit on #5 is the 34C, originally delivered as the 204C in 1956.

Above . . . Milwaukee's *Afternoon Hiawatha* sweeps out of Union Station past a skyline dominated by a Chicago landmark, the huge Merchandise Mart. The four Skytop Lounge cars which graced the *Hiawathas* were built in the railroad's own West Milwaukee Shops in 1948.

Upper right . . . Union Pacific E's 910, 945B and 942B lead the second section of #102/104 past Ogden Tower, just out of its Union Station berth, on a gray September 6, 1965.

Lower right . . . Yellow Milwaukee 31C and mates charge away from Davis Jct., Illinois with #105/111, the combined *City of Portland/City of Denver* on an August 1968 afternoon.

Above . . . On March 30, 1968, all that was left of the one-time parade of passenger trains on the Chicago & North Western's Chicago-Omaha main was three-car #1. Known as the *Kate Shelley 400*, the yellow and green "Streamliner" covered the 138 miles between Chicago and Clinton, Iowa each day. Here 5012B departs Geneva, Illinois with Number 1.

Upper right . . . Number 1's crew is about to receive some orders from the operator in Geneva. EMD 5015B, an E7A, works the afternoon westbound in August 1967.

Lower right . . . North Western's last *Twin Cities 400* departed Chicago on July 23, 1963, ending three decades of operation in the highly competitive market. Assigned as the power for the last #401 were units 5012B and 4052A, pictured here during the station stop at Evanston.

Upper left . . . Between La Fox and Elburn the *Kate Shelley* hustles west toward Iowa in 1968.

Lower left . . . On Sundays and holidays trains 1/2 became 11/12 and operated to Chicago in the late afternoon and west later in the evening, rather than east in the morning and west after the work day. Geneva hosts the 5012B and #12 on a cloudy July 1970 afternoon. Lack of any kind of number boards around the nose made identification of C&NW E's rather difficult.

Above . . . Yellow-nosed 5022B pauses in north suburban Evanston with Chicago-bound #214, the *Bi-Level Peninsula 400.* By the early 1960's most of the North Western's remaining intercity trains to Wisconsin and Upper Michigan were composed of bi-level cars similar in appearance to Chicago push-pull equipment (introduced by the C&NW in 1959). All North Western passenger service outside of Chicago's commute zone expired on April 30, 1971, the day before Amtrak.

Above . . . PA's 67 and 74 have left the snow squalls off Lake Michigan behind as they curve through suburban Lemont in the bright sunshine of January 6, 1968. This is the same train which departed Dearborn in heavy snow an hour earlier (see pages 72/73). American Locomotive built PA's for the Santa Fe in 1946, 1947 and 1948.

Upper right . . . Two weeks later 70 leads a four-car #23 across the Des Plaines River nearing Lemont.

Lower right . . . Classy even on a short train with an all-stops schedule, the distinctive Alco's wore Santa Fe's Warbonnet paint scheme like it was designed for them. Fifty-eight rail miles out of Chicago's Dearborn, 75 is on the point of 23 in Coal City in January 1968. Four of the PA cabs (59, 60, 62 and 66) were sold to the Delaware & Hudson in December 1967. The remaining PA's were retired in 1968 and the first half of 1969.

Above and upper right . . . Last run for the *Chief!* On May 13, 1968, Santa Fe's Number 19 brakes to a stop in Joliet for the last time. Although acknowledging the decline of passenger business and gradually reducing the number of its trains, the AT&SF nevertheless ran all of its remaining schedules in top-notch fashion. The gleaming consist of the last *Chief,* including full-length dome 509, attests to that policy as 19 gathers speed toward the West. Dome-Lounge 509 (series 506-513 by Budd 1954) seated 57 coach and 18 lounge passengers upstairs and 28 lounge patrons downstairs.

Below . . . The very last Santa Fe passenger train in Illinois was eastbound #24 on May 2, 1971. When F7A 344 creeps up to the bumper posts at Dearborn Station in about an hour, it will close the ancient depot forever. Amtrak is already in its second day as 24 departs Joliet.

Above . . . A magnificent red and yellow October sunset is in store for the crew and passengers of Milwaukee/Union Pacific's combined *City of Portland/City of Denver*. UP 941 is the lead locomotive as 105/111 pulls out of Davis Jct., Illinois in 1966.

Upper right . . . Commuter engine 93A teams with E7A 18B to bring the *Sioux* (train 22) into Union Station on a snowy Christmas Day 1965. Normally the 93A would be assigned to Chicago-area suburban trains instead of venturing to Madison, Wisconsin.

Lower right . . . In the aftermath of Chicago's 23-inch blizzard of January 26-27, 1967, Union Pacific 912 creeps between mounds of snow after arriving with a *Cities* train on the 29th. As it was to turn out later, the 912 would be the point unit on the last westbound *Cities* streamliner out of Chicago, train 103 on April 30, 1971, the "City of Everywhere".

Above . . . Number 5, the Milwaukee's *Morning Hiawatha*, grinds out of Union Station on a frigid February 12, 1967. Up front is the 97A (a 1951-built FP7A) destined to also be on the point of the last *Morning Hi* on April 30, 1971.

Below . . . The *Afternoon Hiawatha* hustles away from the Glenview stop on a twelve above zero day in January 1969. A year later, on January 23, 1970, the *Afternoon Hiawathas* made their last runs and the Skytop Lounges were stored.

Above . . . The last passenger is boarding today's Number 17, the westbound *California Zephyr*; in seconds the highball will be given and the pair of E's will have her rolling out of Aurora. Next regular stop—Galesburg—124 miles west.

Probably the least known Chicago passenger trains during the time period of this volume were those of the Soo Line. Operating right into 1965 with standard heavyweight equipment of the pre-stainless steel era, the Soo's varnish nonetheless enjoyed a fine reputation within its somewhat sparsely populated territory.

Lower left . . . Pride of the Soo was its overnight Chicago-Superior (Wisconsin) *Laker*. FP7A 503 and Geeps hustle Number 3 north through the Broadview/Bellwood area in May 1963. Home rails will be reached in a few more miles in Franklin Park.

Upper left . . . Between 1963 and January 1965 the Soo's *Laker* utilized the Illinois Central's downtown station and operated on IC rails to and from west suburban Broadview. GP9's 554, 2552 and 555 bring No. 4 into Central Station in March 1964.

Above . . . Prior to being repainted in red and white, Soo's maroon 554 leads #4 on October 12, 1963. The *Laker* has just pulled into Broadview and will follow IC 4018 and the *Land O'Corn* downtown.

Below . . . The brakeman is poised to line the switches as the inbound *Laker* negotiates the route onto the Illinois Central in Broadview during June 1964.

Last runs for the *Laker*! The Soo closed out its Chicago passenger business in the cold of January 15th and 16th in 1965. Number 3, with GP9 2552 as the point unit, pauses at the Soo's Schiller Park depot with the final Chicago departure on the evening of the 15th, *above*.

Upper left . . . Next morning the last Number 4 arrived behind 554 and 556. Yard workers are bundled against the windswept snow squalls alternating with spots of sunshine as the *Laker* makes its last stop in the Soo's Chicago home, suburban Schiller Park.

Lower left . . . About an hour later the Geeps pull into the IC's Central Station with the last *Laker* of all.

Above . . . One mile west of Leland, 17 is urged across Illinois by a pair of the Burlington's silver E's. Less than a month from this wintry February 1970 afternoon the *CZ* will run no more.

Right . . . A year earlier, on February 18, 1969, the *California Zephyr* speeds west through suburban Lisle behind the 9946A. Included in today's consist are Vista Dome Dormitory-Buffet-Lounge *Silver Lounge* (CB&Q #251) and Dome Obs *Silver Horizon* (CB&Q #375), built by Budd for the *CZ* in 1948. Originally six cars of each of the two types were in *CZ* service. The other five D-B-Lounge cars were *Silver Club* (Q), *Silver Roundup* (Q), *Silver Chalet* (Western Pacific), *Silver Hostel* (WP) and *Silver Shop* (D&RGW). Additional obs cars were *Silver Penthouse* (Q), *Silver Solarium* (Q), *Silver Crescent* (WP), *Silver Planet* (WP) and *Silver Sky* (Denver & Rio Grande Western).

Above . . . Burlington/Great Northern's luxurious *Empire Builder* is being backed into Union Station in April 1963, glistening for its afternoon departure. Q E8A 9973 is in far less glamourous suburban duty on this date, but tomorrow may head one of the Burlington's liners. It was Burlington policy to rotate its E-units between intercity schedules and Chicago commuter work. Great Northern #1255, *Lake of the Woods*, was a 1951-built Dining Car from American Car & Foundry, seating 36 at two and four place tables. Full Length Dome Lounge *Mountain View* (GN 1392) came from Budd in 1955 and was one of six similar eighty-five foot domes built for the *Builder.*

Upper right . . . Great Northern Sleeper *Milk River* cruises through Shabbona, Illinois in the consist of the *Empire Builder.* Pullman-Standard assembled GN 1263 in 1950.

Lower right . . . In west suburban Aurora, a Burlington E stands by in commuter duty as the Big Sky blue *Empire Builder* makes a brief stop in 1969.

In anticipation of the forthcoming merger, two CB&Q E-units were painted in the new Cascade green and white colors chosen for the Burlington Northern. Locomotives 9942 and 9943, ex-CB&Q 9942A and 9943A, were assigned to the point of #31/25 out of Chicago on merger day, March 2, 1970. Later the same month the first two BN passenger units singly lead the same combined *Empire Builder/North Coast Limited.*

Above . . . 9943 rips through west suburban Lisle on the 21st.

Lower right . . . Halfway between Aurora and Sugar Grove, 9942 and two silver companions work their way out of the Fox River valley on the 28th.

Below . . . As passengers detrain from BN's inbound *Denver Zephyr* in Aurora, a Chinese red ex-CB&Q SD9 heads west. The date is July 17, 1970.

Above . . . Two weeks after the merger, Burlington Northern's *Denver Zephyr* still presents an all-stainless steel CB&Q appearance. Westbound between Lisle and Naperville, the Chicago-Denver speedster gleams in a March sunset. *DZ* service continued beyond Amtrak and eventually became the *San Francisco Zephyr.*

THE AMTRAK YEARS—As train-off petitions snowballed into an avalanche in late 1967 and 1968, a ground swell of sentiment to save the passenger train arose across the land and in the halls of Congress. (Most of the public was driving and flying, but apparently the thought of a future without alternatives worried them.) After months of debate, the idea of a National Railroad Passenger Corporation (Railpax) was born in January 1970 as a semi-public corporation established to run the nation's passenger trains. Further wrangling over routes and cities, and the idea itself, continued beyond the October 30th, 1970 signing of the bill into law by President Nixon. Eventually twenty railroads joined Amtrak (as the new corporation eventually was called) in April 1971. Finally, on May 1, 1971, Amtrak assumed control of passenger service on the joining roads.

Above . . . For the first two years of its existence, Amtrak relied (sometimes with unfortunate results) on the locomotives and rolling stock of the rail companies which joined the corporation. Much of this equipment now was over twenty years old, and was badly in need of major work. In March 1972, GM&O 103A leads a two-unit power team curving into Coal City, Illinois on home rails with Amtrak's 302. The consist includes two CB&Q domes and some deadheading baggage cars. 302 is a St. Louis-Chicago run.

Upper right . . . During the latter half of the summer of 1971, one of Amtrak's *Turbo Trains* toured the nation's rails on a publicity jaunt. On September 4th the *Turbo* speeds west beyond Lisle on the Burlington's three-track main in the midst of a heavy shower.

Lower right . . . Well, here we are on the North Western as a C&NW scoot meets a westbound run-through led by Union Pacific 2812, right? Nope! The scene is West Eola and the railroad is the Burlington Northern. UP 2812 (and 3016) are idling on a pig train, waiting for a BN unit to be added on the point. Amtrak's #348, composed of leased C&NW 4088A and two C&NW bilevels, hustles past toward Chicago on September 19, 1973. Between June 1973 and August 1974, North Western F's 4072C, 4075C and 4088A were leased along with bilevel cars for the *Illinois Zephyr*.

Above . . . Burlington Northern's 6455, still in Big Sky blue in November 1973, leads an eastbound setting out at the Nabisco siding, a couple miles west of Naperville. C&NW 4075C and three bilevel coaches zip past, comprising the consist of Amtrak's *Illinois Zephyr.*

Right . . . Three Union Pacific coaches separate the baggage car and a Gulf, Mobile & Ohio diner as Amtrak #1 pauses at Joliet on August 29, 1971. GM&O E7A 100 is up front. Most trains still carry their pre-Amtrak numbers nearly four months after May 1st. Amtrak's first "system" timetable and train renumberings still are to come (in November).

Upper left . . . From the fan's standpoint, Amtrak's early years brought sights of power and equipment showing up in areas away from "home" as Amtrak redistributed some of its inheritances. Racing north on GM&O rails, Amtrak's St. Louis-Chicago 302 hammers the Toledo, Peoria & Western in Chenoa, Illinois behind a Milwaukee Road A-B tandem led by 35C. The date is May 4, 1972.

Lower left . . . In the same summer of 1972 that the Gulf, Mobile & Ohio disappeared as a corporate identity, its E-units reached Milwaukee. On September 9, 1972, GM&O 102A, leased to Amtrak, rolls into the north side of Union Station on MILW iron with Amtrak 326, a Milwaukee-St. Louis run operating *through* Chicago. The GM&O was merged with the Illinois Central on August 10th, one month before 102A brought the *Abraham Lincoln* into the Milwaukee's side of Union Station.

Above . . . EMD 421 idles next to a General Electric P30CH at Amtrak's Chicago terminal in September 1976. The E9A spent most of its career hauling *Cities Streamliners* for the Union Pacific as their 944.

Below . . . Amtrak's #4 still was the *Super Chief/El Capitan* as it rolled into Joliet in August 1973 behind three red-nosed SDP40F's, 524, 522 and 528. During the following winter, the Santa Fe would withdraw consent to use the names and 4 would become the *Southwest Limited*.

Above . . . It's still cool in the shade as a pair of Amtrak's Santa Fe-assigned SDP's, 519 and 526, urge #16 out of North Chillicothe and across the Illinois River. By the time *The Lone Star* reaches Chicago on this July 20, 1974, a sultry summer day will be well underway.

Above . . . On a pleasant summer morning in 1976, General Electric P30CH 722 is in charge of Amtrak 391, destined for Carbondale, Illinois, some 310 miles from Chicago's Union Station. The GE-powered *Shawnee* is curving past the former site of Central Station, now razed to make room for future building along the lakefront.

Above . . . Although popular in the East, the Rail Diesel Car (RDC) could not be considered common in the Midwest. Anywhere from a single car to a half-dozen RDC's were on the roster of about a dozen roads from the Dakotas to Michigan to Oklahoma, but that hardly stacked up against over 100 RDC's on the Boston & Maine for example. Amtrak experimented with RDC's on its Chicago-Dubuque (Iowa) *Blackhawk* run. On April 20, 1975, three of the Budd-built cars work up the leads to Union Station, operating as Amtrak #372. First unit is RDC-1 number 10, formerly Penn Central 36, and originally New Haven 36, built in 1953.

Below . . . Amtrak's first SDP40F poses next to Dome-Parlor-Lounge-Observation Car 9253 at the Santa Fe's 18th Street servicing facility in April 1975. Obs car 9253 was built by the Budd Company in 1952 for *California Zephyr* service as CB&Q 378.

Above . . . In September 1976, SDP40F 508 pulls through the Chicago River bridge (just north of the 21st St. diamonds) during the wyeing of Amtrak's recently-arrived #302, a St. Louis-Chicago schedule on the ICG's ex-GM&O trackage.

Upper left . . . Brand new F40PH 216 and nearly new P30CH 719 pose for a portrait in April 1976. Chicago's Sears Tower looms in the background.

Lower left . . . Twenty-two years after leaving La Grange as Union Pacific 943, Amtrak's 420 handles the head-end spot on #303, bound for St. Louis. Most noticeable change (other than Amtrak's red and silver mist rather than UP's Armour yellow) is the new headlight arrangement.

Above . . . On the first day of June 1975, the *San Francisco Zephyr*, Amtrak #6, thunders out of Aurora on the last lap of its eastbound journey. SDP40F 625, new in 1974, was one of 150 similar EMD's received by Amtrak in 1973-74. The 3000 horsepower cowl units became Amtrak's first ''standard'' locomotive, gradually replacing the fleet of E's chosen from the railroads which joined the NRPC.

Above . . . Fifteen months later, Amtrak 621 passes a reminder of the past as Number 6 slows for the 16th Street curve at Canal Street in Chicago. It already has been five years since the last *North Coast Limited* arrived on these same rails. The *North Coast* name and route continued to surface from time to time during Amtrak's first decade.

In 1973 and again in 1975, Amtrak received a group of power cars, coaches and food service cars built by ANF Frangeco (a French company). Eventually six train sets (twelve power cars) were delivered. At various times these *Turboliners* were installed on Chicago-St. Louis, Chicago-Milwaukee and Chicago to Michigan runs.

Above . . . Power car 64 leads a Detroit and Toledo-bound *Lake Cities* into Porter, Indiana in 1981. The outbound *Turboliner* is operating as Amtrak's #352.

Right . . . During April 1976, Turbo 66 departs Union Station with #354. The French-built Turbos were withdrawn from service in the Midwest in September 1981 and stored for the present at least. High operating costs were cited as the chief reason for the storage of the lightweights, although their inflexible consists (normally the Turbos were run in five-car sets) may have been a contributing factor.

Above . . . The SDP40's leading #48, *The Lake Shore Limited,* clump through the 21st Street switches. The famous junction is only a shadow of its former self on this January 1977 afternoon as many of the tracks have been removed. After completion of the 150 SDP40F's 500-649, a series of derailments led to some uncertainty as to the tracking ability of the SDP on certain curves. Amtrak elected to switch to F40PH's instead in 1977. Over the next four years many of the SDP40F's were traded in for a like number of the 200 and 300 series F40's. Some of the SD's of course had less than five years of service life.

Above . . . Bound for Chicago, the Turbo with power cars 64 and 65 at the ends passes through Porter, Indiana in March 1981. The train is Amtrak's #365, *The Blue Water Limited*, from Port Huron, Michigan, due in Chicago at 11:40.

Below . . . Amply-powered No. 301 skims through the snow at Gardner, Illinois in February 1978. SDP40F 511, originally assigned to Amtrak's Santa Fe trains, and an F40PH should easily bring their three-car Chicago-St. Louis Amfleet train in on time. Trackage is the former Gulf, Mobile & Ohio, now part of the Illinois Central Gulf.

Above . . . Late on a September afternoon, Amtrak 206 hauls #381, the *Illini*, up the incline which will carry it over the BN and the Chicago River. In less than a mile the Amfleet train will reach ICG rails and set a southerly course toward Champaign-Urbana.

Upper left . . . Power car 62 swings around the curve at Porter, Indiana and heads for Michigan with *Turboliner #352*.

Lower left . . . As the Valparaiso, Indiana arrival and departure board indicates, Amtrak also is in the commuter business out of Chicago. The ex-Pennsy rush hour trains were being handled by P30CH's and bi-levels in 1981.

Upper left . . . A single F40 wheels Amtrak #21 south across the Kankakee River in Wilmington, Illinois. On this October 1977 morning the 237 was one of the newer Amtrak F40PH's.

Lower left . . . A westbound Santa Fe freight led by SD40 5015 is being held north of the Joliet Union Station as Amtrak 319 brings #303 into the depot. Shortly Amtrak will be off for St. Louis and the Santa Fe will resume its journey to Kansas City on this hot July 1981 afternoon.

Above and below . . . Three F40PH's lead No. 3 out of the bridge across the Chicago Sanitary and Ship Canal and into Lemont on July 2, 1981. By late 1981, F40PH deliveries to Amtrak had reached nearly 200 units (200-390). Following the trio of F40's on the *Southwest Limited* is a consist of Superliner cars. The long awaited long-distance cars, originally ordered in 1975, finally were placed in service beginning in late 1979 through early 1981. Closest to the camera are Coach Baggage cars in the 31000 series.

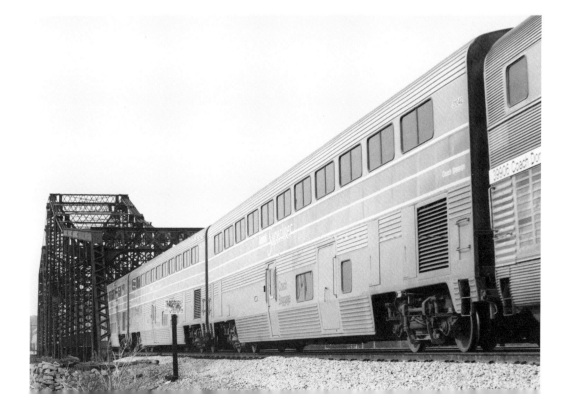

At the time of this writing it has been over 16 years since Santa Fe PA number 60, carrying green, strode across the 21st Street diamonds in June 1965 with First 23, the *Grand Canyon*. The luxurious 1950's era of the streamlined train, complete with domes, diners and Pullmans, already had been declining through the mid-1960's. With the passenger train near death by 1971, Amtrak arrived on the scene. Although marked by a series of ups and downs, Amtrak's first decade overall was upbeat into mid-1980. Recent setbacks have clouded the future outlook for the passenger train, and it seems obvious that the great years of the *Century*, of *Zephyrs*, *Hiawathas* and *Chiefs*, will not return. One can only hope that Chicago's (and the nation's) passenger trains will find plenty of green boards in Amtrak's second decade.